How to Select and Perform Monologues

Acting One Series

VOLUME 1

Frank Catalano

Lexington Avenue Press
Copyright © 2017 Frank Catalano
All rights reserved.
ISBN: 0692784780
ISBN-13: 9780692784785

How to Select and Perform Monologues

TABLE OF CONTENTS

BASIC TERMINOLOGY

PRACTICE MONOLOGUES

Introduction

As an author, I have written several monologue books including ***ART OF THE MONOLGUE*** and ***WHITE KNIGHT BLACK NIGHT*** – both of which focused on the performance of a monologue as an artistic work. This current volume focuses on the presentation of monologues specifically for the purpose of auditions and acting classes. The difference here is that the actual selection and presentation of the material is focused more upon the actor's abilities and type than the performance or the material. Why short monologues? As an acting teacher, I have always advised my students ***"less is more."*** What does that actually mean? In this case, I want the actor to focus specifically on a given purpose in the presentation of each piece. The given purpose of an audition is to provide the auditioner a sample of your acting abilities, demeanor, ability to take direction and ultimately to determine whether or not you are the right fit for what they are looking for. But, lets be honest, a casting director is rarely if ever going to have you perform a monologue if they are reading people for a specific role. They will just have you perform the actual lines of the character that you are reading for. So what would be the purpose of a monologue? In a larger sense, a director of a theatre company, a university theatre school, an agent or manager might want to see how you perform prepared material. They would want to see how you create the moment without external direction so they can have an idea of the kind of actor you really are. To accomplish this, you need to present something that's brief, to the point and gives them an idea of who you are and what you can do. They don't need the whole performance, just a sample. An actor should have at least two short contemporary monologues (one comedy and one dramatic) ready to go at all times. If you want to be totally prepared you can add at least one or two short classical monologues to your acting arsenal. But here's the rub. If you prepare, well-known material from familiar sources, most auditioners will have seen and heard other actors do these same monologues. Here, you run the danger of comparison. As you perform, they will be thinking about the last person that presented the same material. How did they do it? How does the interpretation you are presenting differ? Which one is better? You don't want them thinking about anything other than you. To hedge your bet, you should select monologues that are new and fresh to their ear. Show them something new that is a perfect fit for just you. Something, that they can only imagine you performing. It should show what you can do emotionally, intellectually and physically and most importantly be brief and to the point. Brief and to the point means about one to two minutes. Remember, a class or audition presentation is a sample of what you can do, not the whole performance. If they want a whole performance, they need to cast you or buy a ticket.

Shorter monologues are also great to use within an acting class. Like an audition, you want to bring into the class a short sample of your acting ability or to showcase a specific aspect of your talent. If your strong suit is emotional roles, prepare a short emotional monologue. If it's physicality, then prepare something that relies centrally upon your ability to move within the space. This is no secret. Acting teachers and students prefer shorter monologues for class presentations. Why? This allows both the teacher and the student the ability to focus on specific acting issues rather than restating them over and over again within a cumbersome presentation. Usually, an acting teacher (just like a casting director) pretty much knows what they need to work on with you after the first minute of your presentation. So, why not dazzle them with a presentation that's short and sweet. Give just enough to make them interested but leave them wanting for more. If you can do that, you are where you need to be.

This book contains seventy individual monologues that can be performed by male or female characters. There is an equal mix of comedy and drama and all are within the one to two minute time range. You might be thinking, which one is right for me? Find a piece that you can closely connect to either on an emotional or intellectual level. Put yourself in the space as the character and let the monologue do the rest of the work. Ultimately, the right monologue for you is one that they have never seen that showcases your unique talents. Think of an audition monologue as a means to end. As an audition piece, it's going to exhibit what you can do and where you would fit in to a particular company or agent roster. As a class exercise it's going to give your acting teacher a specific insight about who you are, your talents and what areas of acting you need to work on.

Lastly, monologues like everything else, are subject to our tastes and needs at any given moment. Don't be afraid to try many different monologues as your creative growth progresses or you feel you need to do something different. Make this book your source for the magic that you will do. Go back to it again and again whenever you feel there is a need for it.

What Is A Monologue?

The American Heritage Dictionary defines a monologue as a long speech made by one person, often monopolizing a conversation. You may be thinking, I already know that, tell me something I don't know. Okay, a monologue when spoken can reveal a small part of a character's soul. Think of those thoughts in which you have spoken aloud to someone or yourself. The words you speak come from within you and have special meaning. Unless, you count as monologues leaving phone messages, placing an order at the automated machine at Jack in the Box or trying to talk on the phone to customer service at a bank. It is true that a monologue is a speech made by one person but really it is a lot more than just that. What the person says in his/her speech should be worthy of speech itself to be considered a monologue. What am I saying? It should be a speech connected in some core way to a character's intellectual, emotional, spiritual and physical state. If it is not that, then it is not a monologue. It is whatever it is: leaving a phone message, ordering a cheeseburger or trying to find out why a check has bounced.

Within the framework of a performing arts presentation, a monologue is one person speaking for an extended period alone or with other characters upon the stage or within a camera shot. The speech can be the character's thoughts spoken aloud to himself or herself, to another character, to the audience or an object or entity. How a monologue is presented has a lot to do with the reality of the universe the character lives in and to a greater extent the point of view or creative framework of the presentation. I am defining point of view as **how** a creative work is presented to its audience. Several years ago, I attended a production of

William Shakespeare's Hamlet at small theatre in Los Angeles. I sat in the first row about three feet from the actor who played Hamlet as he uttered those famous lines **"To be or not to be..."** I had experienced this soliloquy dozens of times before within a representational framework where the Hamlet character reveals his inner thoughts by speaking to himself out loud. In this particular production, the actor who played Hamlet turned toward me and asked the famous question, **"To be or not to be?"** At first I wanted to blurt out like Robert Di Niro in **Taxi Driver, "Are you talking to me?"** But, somehow thought it might not be appropriate. So I said nothing. But, I did give him a look of acknowledgment. As if to say **"I heard that... and that is definitely a question to consider."** For the rest of the show, the audience kept looking at me as if they wanted me to do or say something. I never did. I am not saying that it was wrong to present the Hamlet soliloquy in this manner. The creative framework of that particular production of Hamlet was centered on the characters (including Hamlet) acknowledging the presence of the audience. At that particular performance, I unwittingly assumed that role. I could have chosen to respond verbally to Hamlet, but I chose just to acknowledge his look. However, we can say that Hamlet acknowledging the audience in the middle of his soliloquy was done on purpose and was part of the creative framework of the presentation. The creative framework, which defines a presentation of a play or film to an audience, usually falls within the point of view of the Director.

The Director sets the framework and tone of how the material will be presented. When you choose to perform a particular monologue, just like a director, you must choose **how** you will convey the reality of your character and situation to an audience. You must ask yourself, what do I want to achieve within my creative framework and what is the desired outcome? I am not suggesting that you perform your audition monologue directly to an auditioner. I think it is best to create a framework that keeps them separate from the reality of your character. This allows them the freedom to make notes on your performance, sit back and see what you can do. You don't want them; feeling forced to react to your gaze or directed line toward them. It will make them uncomfortable and lessen your chance to showcase what you can do. Your creative framework in presenting a monologue should be focused on how to best present the reality of the character you have created and to connect that character to your individual talents. The purpose of an audition monologue is not to solely entertain, it is to show how you create a character, interpret lines and present them to an audience.

Now that we have discussed what a monologue is and how it should be presented, let's get back to our original question. Why do we have to do monologues anyway?

Why Do I Have To Do A Monologue?

Most casting directors, when reading actors for a particular project, like to have the work performed from a specific script either as a cold reading or a memorized screen test. So having one or more monologues prepared is not going to land you a specific role in a film or television program. In order to do that, you are going to have to do a *cold reading* of the material from the project. If you cannot use a monologue for a film or television audition, why bother working on one?

The answer to the question of why we do monologues is to be able to show a casting person, agent or performing arts school representative our ability to perform prepared (rather than cold) material and offer such monologues within a clear-cut presentational format. In this book, I have developed primarily shorter pieces to be used for auditions and acting classes. In a classroom / studio setting, an actor can work on specific challenges of character creation, line memorization, nervousness and physicality. As an audition piece, the performer wants to present a monologue that is a concise sample of his/her work which highlights their ability to memorize dialogue, create the intellectual, emotional, physical and spiritual state of a character. It should also exhibit the actor's creative ability to present prepared material from a specific point of view. The *"how" and "why"* we do monologues then is clear. This is a sample of how you can interpret material when you have had a time to prepare it and present it within a specific creative framework. However, just because it is prepared, you are not expected to create a whole play. What is expected is for you to provide a short sample (one to two minutes) of your creativity and talent to a specific audience. Who is this audience? It can be an agent, producer, and an artistic director of a theatre ensemble, an admissions committee at an acting school/college or a director. However, the **who** is not as important as the **how** you create it. The first step in this process is the selection of the right material.

How Do I Select A Monologue That's Right For Me?

By Casting Type

No matter how versatile you think you may be as a performer, a casting director or agent will only see you playing roles that they feel fall within your appropriate casting type. Casting type is a combination of factors, which can include age, physical stature, hair color, ethnicity, speech patterns or accent and generally the way you appear to most people most of the time. You want to select a monologue that is **type appropriate** for you. That is, if you are female age twenties, you should not select a character that is an older woman. Pick a character that is generally your own age. Agents and casting directors will look to identify you in one type category or another.

By talent and skills

If you are preparing a monologue for an audition for entrance into a school or theatre ensemble, you want to select material that will highlight what you do the best. If you have difficulty in showing intense emotion, then stay away from those types of monologues until you can perfect the skill to perform them. Select monologues that will highlight what you do best. Note that some schools require selection of monologues from existing plays either from a specific list or within a date range. For example, they may request preparation of two monologues: one classical such as Shakespeare, Moliere, or Sophocles and one contemporary within the last fifty years. If you are doing a short monologue for a commercial agent, select something contemporary no longer than two minutes. If you feel your strongest talent is comedy, then lead with that. If you feel your strongest talent is drama, then lead with that. Often, when you are requested to do two, they will have you perform the first one and then tell you the second monologue is not necessary. This does not mean that you have done a poor job. It just means that they have seen what they need to see.

Compatibility with career or artistic goals

Select monologues that are compatible with the goals you are attempting to achieve. If you audition for a commercial agent, a crisp, short, high-energy (but not too happy) monologue would probably be best. A longer dramatic narrative or verse monologue would not be the best choice for a commercial agent, but may work in perfectly for an audition for a theatrical agent (film and television), theater company or college performing arts program.

Purpose or Skill Goal

An acting teacher may ask you to select a monologue, so that you can work on a specific acting goal such as anger, physicality or listening. For example, if you are asked to work on a specific emotion, select a monologue that will stretch your abilities in that area.

Treat Your Monologue As If It Were A Scene

Many actors hate performing monologues because they feel it is just a speech and not a true representation of their acting ability. They believe that performing a monologue does not provide the opportunity to show a casting director or agent the actor's ability to react to another character. We have stated earlier that a monologue is a longer speech where a character can speak to himself or herself, another character or object or the audience. When you create a monologue know **who** you are talking to and don't forget to create their presence for the audience. Your monologue dialogue should not be just a wall-to-wall recitation of lines but instead a well thought out pattern of dialogue, which takes into consideration the intellectual, emotional, physical and spiritual universe of the character.

Let's stop here a moment and define these four character attributes.

Intellectual:

This is what your character intellectually believes within his/her universe. It goes to the core of the things they do. It could be as simple as Democrat or Republican but it can go deeper about their understanding of the world they live in. Characters are often thrust into situations that force them to make decisions based upon logic rather than emotion. This is often the case in business decisions where statistics or numbers are involved. However, an intellectual choice can also be based upon a belief system within the character. Some factor causes them to calculate and then act upon a decision that is centered on facts and data rather than feelings.

Emotional:

This is what your character feels about themselves and the other character they relate to in their universe. What emotion dominates their existence and how does it effect what they do and what happens to them. Certain situations demand an emotional response. What your character feels becomes more important than what they think or intellectually rationalize in a given situation. In 1916, there was a shark attack on a little boy in an inland Florida lagoon. It was unbelievable to think that a shark would swim that far inland from the ocean. But it happened. As the shark attacked the seven year old, an adult man jumped into the water and attempted to pull him to safety. The shark killed them both, but there is more to it than that. The underlying motivation for the rescuer was to save the boy despite the danger of being torn apart himself. Perhaps it was fear itself that drew the man into the water. In either case, it was a totally emotional response.

Physical:

How does your character physically interact with the universe they live in? How do they move? How do they interact physically with other characters? Much of our physical response to the world is filtered through our culture and the times we live in. You could be on a subway car in New York City just inches away from another individual. Actually so close to them that you could smell what they ate for breakfast and not think anything of it because the physicality of that space and situation makes it so. You could take the same physical situation and place it on a line at the supermarket in Los Angeles and you would perceive anyone that close to you as invading your space. A character's physical interaction with the universe that surrounds them can also be influenced by culture or time period. What is acceptable in one culture or time period may not be acceptable in another.

Spiritual:

This goes beyond religious conviction to the core of a character's belief system. Your character's moral core and how they perceive what is right and wrong within their universe. Certain characters find themselves on a journey of discovery and their motivation is centered on that journey. Certainly, Don Quixote's quest in Man of La Mancha would be an example. But, your character doesn't have to be on a life long quest to find the meaning of life to have a spiritual motivation. The spirituality can simply be an exploration of aspect of your character's inner being.

Certainly, try to allow whom ever your character is speaking to react to what is being conveyed just as you would in a two-person scene. Your character speaks the lines in the monologue and then allows the other character or the audience to respond. Even if they are not making a sound, you need to give them time to react. If you do this, your presentation will be more than a mere recitation of the words of the script in which you race through the lines before you forget them. Allow whomever you are speaking absorb what you are saying and doing. In addition, don't forget to create them in the space. Look at them, react to them and allow them to react to what your character is doing within the piece.

What's The Best Way To Memorize My Lines And Create A Physical Life For My Character?

I have heard many actors complain: *"I knew the lines outside but now, on the stage, I just can't remember anything."* When I hear this type of statement, I know what they have forgotten to do is create a physical life for their character. They fall into the trap of thinking about a monologue as just a speech rather than a slice of a character's life. This means that the monologue should be more than a character speaking. When preparing to perform a monologue don't forget to create the physical life of the character. What I mean is the physical connection to where your character is and what they are doing as they speak. Creating a physical life will go a long way in helping you to memorize the lines. The ability to memorize what your character is saying will be connected to a specific physical reality and idea. Your brain will connect what is being said to a specific movement and place. However, you cannot move without purpose. What kind of universe does your character live in and how do they move within it? A character's universe has everything to do with the actual space from which they speak, the time period they live in and *who* they are speaking with. If a monologue is a soliloquy, which takes place in a graveyard, and the character is speaking aloud to no one is different from a speech talking to a best friend over a cup of coffee.

Performing A Monologue For An Audition - How To Create An Implementation Strategy

Think of an implementation strategy as a plan to create a frame or foundation to build your monologue. The implementation strategy becomes the concept for presentation. Whatever the purpose of your monologue the preparation for presentation should include an implementation strategy. You may think it is the director's job to create the framework of the character's physicality and emotion and that you should not have to concern yourself with the details of how it will be presented. The truth is that the *who and the how* are indelibly connected. It is like the chef who labors over the preparation and ingredients making up a particular dish, forgetting presentation and just throwing his creation onto a paper plate. In that very act, the chef negates the creative process that taken place before. An actor is no different; consideration of presentation is just as important as character preparation. While an actor cannot control all aspects of presentation, the development of an implementation strategy will create a foundation for the actor to rely upon.

Creating A Performance Dynamic – How To Make A Creative Box To Play In

The dynamic of any presentation takes into consideration all of the physical characteristics of the performance space, the performer's relationship to that space, the distance of the intended audience to the performer, the composition of the intended audience, the surrounding reality of the performance and ultimately the purpose of the performance itself. The dynamics of any given performance can change as the physical characteristics of the space change. While it is virtually impossible for any performer to know totally the dynamic of every audition performance in advance, it is possible to develop a strategy of presentation, based upon what elements are available.

For an audition, you can only assume the dynamics of the space and distance to the intended audience. You might be asked to present a monologue in an office setting, a conference room, or an empty stage. The best strategy is to develop a plan for all three and be prepared for any variation you might encounter. In an audition dynamic, the person you are auditioning for may be looking for a specific element and not your total performance. They also may be multi tasking (making notations, conferring with an associate or looking at your resume) while you are in the midst of your performance. Lastly, the reality you attempt to create might be interrupted by an outside source such as a telephone, people entering the space or the casting person themselves.

How To Play Each Moment As If It Were Part Of A Larger Mosaic

The **Presentation Dynamic** is literally the creative box you get to play in. It is the creative framework, which is made up of your character's world, and the actual physical elements within the specific performance environment all rolled into one. It could be a stage, a camera angle, a casting office, or on set location that your character must evolve within. Once you have established this creative framework, there is a multitude of possibilities that are present within that dynamic at that particular moment in time.

Using "What If?"

You have made the choices detailing **who, what, where and when**. Now, let your character consider: *"What If"* one of these choices weren't so? Example: You are Romeo quietly watching Juliet standing on her balcony.

Who: A Montague (who falls in and out love) and enemy of the Capulet's

What: Spying upon Juliet as she speaks her private thoughts

Where: The Capulet's orchard, Verona - a place he should not be.

When: Nighttime after the Capulet feast.

Romeo sees the love of his life but cannot muster the will to speak. As she speaks each line, he falls deeper and deeper into silence. He succumbs to his fear and gets up to run away when at the last possible moment, despite his fear, he hears Juliet say:

Romeo, doff thy name,

And for that name which is no part of thee

Take all myself!

When Romeo hears this, his fear, vanishes in an instant, and he speaks! Why? He knows he can get it all.

I take thee at thy word:

Call me but love, and I'll be new baptized;

Henceforth I never will be Romeo

Using the "**What if**," you are choosing to play the moment as if this time it will be different. You are playing this scene and speech as if he were going to walk away and somehow this play, at this moment in time is different than any other that has happened before. The key to playing the "**what if**" is that a character must believe it and more importantly the audience must believe that the **"what if"** is going to change the outcome. Fight the logical inclination to say to yourself, **this is Shakespeare or this is the text, it cannot be changed**. I am not suggesting a change in text, only a change in intention. We often play the end of the scene because there is a preconceived notion by both performers and audiences as to how it all turns out. We need to recreate that notion in the form of "**what if**." Let the audience sit on the edge of their seats and wonder if that maybe just this time, at this moment, Romeo just might walk away. What would happen then? Using this approach makes your work unpredictable and interesting.

How To Create The "Moment Before"

Where have you come from and what has just happened the moment before?

Within the reality of your character, what moment has the character just left before they entered the moment of your monologue? What was significant about that moment and how has the moment before influenced the intellectual, emotional, physical and spiritual state of your character during the monologue? Within this creative framework, the actor then can convey the thoughts of the character, as they would appear in the full presentation of the work. Playing the moment before the lights go up or the camera rolls then allows the audience to catch your character in the midst of their existence living their life in its entirety.

How To Create "Now" Using Objectives And Specific Beats

What is your character's main objective?

By speaking the words of the monologue and living the moment, what does your character desire to have happen when they finish speaking? Ask yourself, *why* is my character saying and doing this? What is your character's desired outcome?

What are your character's sub objectives? Mark them as individual beats.

Are there smaller objectives or beats that your character must overcome in order to achieve their main objective? A beat could be a small section of the dialogue or movement within the monologue. Create a series of beats within your monologue to identify your sub objectives. For example, what would Romeo's sub objectives be?

Beat #1   Romeo sees the love of his life but cannot muster the will to speak.

Beat #2   As she speaks, he succumbs to his fear and gets up to run away.

Beat #3   At the last possible moment, despite his fear, he hears Juliet say:

Romeo, doff thy name,

And for that name which is no part of thee

Take all myself!

Beat #5   He stops. When Romeo hears this, his fear, vanishes in an instant.

Beat #6   He speaks.

I take thee at thy word:

Call me but love, and I'll be new baptized;

Henceforth I never will be Romeo

What are the obstacles in the way of achieving your objectives?

In the course of events leading up to, during and after the completion of the monologue, can you identify any obstacles, which are preventing your character from achieving his/her desired goals? Are these obstacles generated externally (literally physical elements) or internal (obstacles created from within your character) which prevent them from their objective? Identify these obstacles and create ways to acknowledge and overcome them.

What is going on at this moment?

At the very moment the monologue begins, what is actually happening? If you took a snapshot of this moment, what would be its title? If you enter the your home holding a bouquet of flowers, kiss your wife and hand them to her, and then after giving them to her, you tell her that you have lost your job, what is the title you would place under this moment? It can be called many things, perhaps *"losing my job"* or *"loss"* but it would not be called *"Handing her the bouquet"* because that action is not what is really going on. It is just an action, which is part of the overall moment. Consider what is *really* going on in your character's universe at the moment the monologue begins.

When is this moment in time?

Once you have established what the true moment is, then address the question is *"when"* is it? Using the example described above, the moment can be described as morning, day or night but more helpful would be the moment after I lost my job or late at night after I have been walking for hours, because I didn't know how I would tell you. It is literally a definition of *"now."* Once you understand this, you will know what to play. But also understand that *"now"* is constantly changing as the moment evolves.

Where are you? What is the space for your character?

Even though you may perform a monologue in any number of nondescript spaces, make a decision for your character about specifically where this moment is taking place. Is it at home, on the bus, in an elevator, on a podium in front of a thousand spectators? What is the space? Is it small and confined, larger than life or somewhere in between? Do not confuse this with the Dynamic of Performance (that is more concerned with the physical properties of the performance space) the *"where are you"* question addresses solely the reality of the character's universe rather than the performance space. Make specific decisions about the space your character occupies when they begin to move and speak.

How To Create The "Moment After"

Where are you going?

If a character is in a particular space in a particular moment, where will they go next? Is it somewhere specific? Create a concept of motion. Let the words in the monologue and the physical life you have in the moments you create propel you to the next.

Everybody likes to know where they have been and where they are going.

I am not asking you to predict the future. However, your character and the audience, in a larger sense, should have some idea about where they going intellectually, emotionally physically and spiritually as a result of the monologue being spoken. Everybody loves to peer into the future and know even briefly, what the next moment will bring. Even if you don't really have a clear-cut idea of all of it, give your character and your audience a taste of what may come next. An audience, will say, *"Okay, I have watched and listened to you, now what's going to happen?"* Answer the question: *"Now that I have spoken these words, this is what's going to happen next."* You have to show them how it's going to be and take them along with you on your journey.

"What has happened during this journey?" After all that has been said, has your character changed? If your character has spoken aloud to himself or herself another character or the audience, has this auditory expression of their inner thoughts changed them in anyway? It may be a minute change, but it is a change nonetheless. What happens next? You as

the performer and your character have to answer the question: How has the universe changed and because of that change what will happen next? You do not have to write new lines to the monologue but there has to be a sense that something will follow.

How do you play this?

We have come full circle. A character must have some resolve intellectually, emotionally, physically and spiritually that connects to what is going on within their universe.

How do you show this?

The way a character contemplates on what they have just spoken in the monologue, or how they react emotionally, or how they physically accommodate the change. A monologue does not end when the character utters the last line. It ends when the audience experiences the character's reaction to the last line. The audience wants a sense of the significance of what has transpired and glimpse of what will be. That is what keeps them invested in your character, they want to know and be part of what is going to happen next.

When Macbeth speaks the last few lines of his soliloquy, the audience has had a glimpse of his tormented soul and has seen the shadow of the murder that is to come.

Macbeth

I have no spur to prick the sides of my intent, but only vaulting ambition, which o'erleaps itself and falls on the other

When Macbeth utters the last line "**And falls on the other**," the very moment after, we see the murder that is to take place within his eyes. He exits with a resolve that is clear to us all when he walks off the stage. The audience knows, he has changed and because of this resolution, something significant is going to happen. He is going to kill the king and we have witnessed the creation of this decision.

How To Begin A Monologue At An Audition

You have done your preparation, what about the audition itself? When you enter the audition space, get a sense of the room. What is the energy level of the people inside? Where are they sitting? In front of you, on the side or both? How large is the space? What is the distance between where you will perform and the people watching you? What is the acoustic quality of the space? Where is the light and are there any seats or other set materials in the space? Adjust to any deficiencies on the fly. If it is a stage and there is an object in your way from a previous audition, it is okay to use it or move it out of the way. Try to make the space as accommodating as you can for the performance. Make the space your own as you create the universe of the character.

If you are required to speak before, you perform the monologue or do a verbal set up which might include the monologue title and a little bit of background about the source material and setting, try to be as concise as possible. Try not to use words like *"um" or "like."* Instead, be very specific and state the name of the source material and a short summary of the portion of the source material that you are performing and what (if anything) is unique about it. You can prepare this in advance and memorize as part of the overall presentation. If the situation calls for you to go right into the monologue take your time to create the universe that the character lives in. Once it is time to start the actual performance portion of your audition, make sure you allow some time to separate the reality of the *"audition"* and the reality of the *"universe of the character"* you are to perform. Don't be a ***good soldier*** and go directly from an interview into a character. You will not totally achieve the transition and your performance will seem uneven and full of distractions. Before you speak, take a moment to let your character's universe surround you. Don't do warm ups, stretch out or lower your head toward the floor as you **get into character** then suddenly face forward as the character in a totally different physicality. This caveat may seem elementary but I have seen actors do it all the time.

Remember that a monologue, from a presentational perspective, does not begin with the first line. It begins with the moment before the first line, which causes the character to say those words. A monologue can even begin with a physical action or creation of an emotional or physical state by the character. If you are playing Hamlet, ask yourself what causes this character to speak the line **"To be or not to be..."** He just doesn't speak those words because Shakespeare wrote them. There is an underlying moment that occurs before the lines are spoken that drives the character to speak those words. When a character speaks those first words of a monologue, let them be a reaction to a previous intellectual, emotional or physical moment. This can be a previous moment in the play, film, or something the audience has not even seen. How you play this reaction to a previous moment has all to do with your character's intellectual, emotional, physical and spiritual connection. Ask yourself, what does my character **"think"** about this situation, how does my character **"feel"** right now and how does my character respond **"physically"** to this place and situation at hand. And what are your character's beliefs about the nature of their universe and what is right and what is wrong? Once you have answers to these questions, you will have something to play.

Where Should I Look When I Perform An Audition Monologue?

A character can speak to themselves aloud, to another character or to the audience. However, most individuals involved within the casting selection process do not like to be included in the reality of the presentation. They want to be free to make notes and just experience what you are doing. Some acting teachers direct their students to speak **over the heads** of their audience. I don't like this practice because it is distracting to watch and does not allow the person watching your audition to connect to your character. Better, if you are performing your monologue as a soliloquy, direct your comments and actions to yourself. If you are speaking to another character, create an on stage space for that character that the auditioner can easily see. This can be an empty space on the stage or a chair or set piece. If you are addressing the audience, create a similar empty space or spaces within the audience area. In this way, the auditioner can choose to participate when they want to but also be free to look down and make notes about you or your performance. Ultimately, I am not one for rules, if you perform your monologue directly to the auditioner, you will not fall through a hole in the floor. You can do anything you want to do to create the best reality for your specific monologue.

How Do I End My Audition Monologue?

In a typical stage production setting, when a monologue is completed the lights might fade or another character might speak. In a film, another character can speak; they could cut to the next scene or fade to black. In an audition setting, you will not have any control over the space in which you will perform. There may be harsh lighting; exterior noise or it may not be a performance space at all. I have seen several methods of ending a monologue that I suggest that *you not do.* The first, at the end of the monologue, the actor just bows their head toward the floor as if to say, *"its over – you can applaud now."* As you can imagine this unnatural ending is abrupt and solicits an artificial applause and response from your auditioner. Applause belongs in a theatre performance, not an audition. The second method, at the end of the monologue the actor says the word *"scene."* This is a verbal cue spoken to the auditioner indicating that the monologue is over. This method is unnatural and creates an abrupt almost jarring quality in the presentation. In addition, actors who use this declaration method of ending have a tendency to physically comment upon their work when they say *"scene."* They complete their monologue and then in a very different physicality smile and shrug their shoulders upward in apology then say *"scene."* This is not a monologue ending; it is an apology. It is as if the actor says to the auditioner, *"I'm so sorry for making you sit through this awful monologue."* All of these artificial methods don't allow the monologue to end naturally. What then, should you do?

If we operate on the assumption that you are not directly addressing the auditioner during the monologue presentation, then ending your monologue is very simple. You complete the last line or action of the monologue and then allow a moment after to occur. This allows both the audience and whomever your character is speaking to react to that last moment. You take this short beat, then change your physicality from that of the character **back** to your own or neutral position and look directly at and acknowledge the auditioner. This will tell them that the reality created for the character has now ended and that you are back at the audition. You don't ask for applause or any reaction for that matter.

All you are communicating to the auditioner is that the monologue presentation is now over. The auditioner normally will say **"thank you"** and that is it. They may comment on your performance, give specific notes or ask you additional questions. Remember, it is not a good idea to comment on your own performance because it is a losing proposition either way. If you say, **"Wow, that was terrible. I can't believe how bad that was."** They may not have felt that way. Alternatively, if you say, **"Wow, was that hot or what? I can't believe how well I just nailed it today."** In this case, they may also not agree. Best bet is to not comment at all and let them do the talking. If you are asked to perform portions again and are given notes, listen to those notes carefully and try to incorporate them into your second performance. Many times an auditioner will give notes just to see how you take direction and incorporate their comments into your performance.

How To Have Fun At An Audition

This last note will sound a bit cliché' but if you are having a good time at your audition, the person watching and listening to you will be more likely to become engaged in the intellectual, emotional, physical and spiritual life of your character. In addition, if you feel good about what you are doing, you will do it better. Can you visualize that first moment you had the thought that you wanted to be an actor? Maybe you were watching television, a movie or a play. You sat in your seat and you thought to yourself.

"I'd like to do that! I want to be up there on the screen or on the stage. I want to do it because it's something I would enjoy. No it's something that I would love. I love to act because it's inside of me and part of who I am. I can't think of doing anything else!"

Okay, so that seems a bit over the top. But didn't you ever feel this way at least a little bit. Well, I want you to go back to that personal moment for you. Go back to it and remember that you want to act because you love it and it makes you happy when you do it. Keep that always in your heart and find joy in what you do. Even if you don't get the part or you get it wrong, it doesn't matter. There will always be another day, another audition and another part to play. When you audition or perform in class, have a great time. Be thankful that you have the opportunity to perform and share your talent. This is not really advice, its common sense. But it goes to the core of why we act. We act because we love to act and that passion should be part of everything that we do.

Where Can I Find A Monologue That's Right For Me?

There are many free on line sources for monologues from both stage and film projects. I have listed several sources here.

WEBSITES

Actorama	http://www.actorama.com/monologues/
Best Film Speeches and Monologues	http://www.filmsite.org/bestspeeches.html
Daily Actor - Free Monologues from Movies and Plays	http://www.dailyactor.com/contemporary-monologues/
Drama Bookshop	http://www.dramabookshop.com
Drew's Script-o-Rama	http://www.script-o-rama.com/
Instant Monologues	https://www.instantmonologues.com
Internet Broadway Database	https://www.ibdb.com
Internet Movie Database	http://www.imdb.com
Internet Movie Script Database	http://www.imsdb.com/
Lortel Archives – Internet Off-Broadway Database	http://www.lortel.org/Archives
Monologue Archive	http://www.monologuearchive.com
Monologue Genie	http://www.monologuegenie.com/about.html
Not My Shoes – Monologue Index	http://notmyshoes.net/monologues/
Play Database	http://www.playdatabase.com
Playbill Vault	http://www.playbill.com/vault

Shakespeare Monologues	http://www.shakespeare-monologues.org
Simply Scripts	http://www.simplyscripts.com/
Stage Agent	http://stageagent.com/monologues
The Broadway League	https://www.broadwayleague.com/home/
Theatre History – Archive	http://www.theatrehistory.com/plays/monologues.html
Why Insanity.com	http://ww34.whyinsanity.com/

In addition, there monologue book collections that contain original material or selections from plays and movies. These books can be found for free at local and school libraries or purchased online at sites such as Amazon.com, Barnes and Noble or Kobo Books. They can be purchased in hard copy form or as digital downloads. I am listing the three monologue books that I have authored which contain original monologues.

ART OF THE MONOLOGUE – Monologues They Haven't Heard Yet
Author Frank Catalano
Lexington Avenue Press
(A collection of fifty original monologues)

WHITE KNIGHT BLACK NIGHT – Short Monologues for Auditions
Author Frank Catalano
Lexington Avenue Press
(A collection of fifty short original monologues)

SHORT MONOLOGUES FOR AUDTIONS
Author Frank Catalano
Lexington Avenue Press
(A collection of original monologues for auditions)

BASIC TERMINOLOGY

BASIC TERMINOLOGY FOR PERFORMING ON STAGE

THEATRE – WHO'S WHO IN PRODUCTION

BOX OFFICE

Personnel who are located in a place at a theater where tickets are bought or reserved.

DESIGNERS

The people who create the "universe" of the play including sound, lighting, costume, setting, props and special effects.

DIRECTOR

The person, who provides the point of view for the presentation of the play and directs the action.

HOUSE MANAGER

Runs all aspects of the theatre outside of the production including box office, audience and lobby area.

PLAYWRIGHT

A person who writes (DESCRIPTION, ACTION, DIALOGUE) in the form of a play to be presented orally or on stage.

STAGE MANAGER/PRODUCTION MANAGER

The person in charge of all elements of a play during the run of a performance.

TECHNICAL DIRECTOR

The senior technical person within the production unit.

PERFORMING ARTS PRESENTATION SPACE

STAGING TYPES

PROSCENIUM:

The performer "P" is on one side and the audience 'A' is on another. Ideal for plays which require extensive sets and back drops. Example: The Kennedy Center in Washington D.C.

THRUST

The performer "P" has the audience "A" on three sides. There is some limitation to the kinds of sets that can be used because of site lines. There is increased audience interaction. Example: Mark Taper Forum in Los Angeles

ARENA OR ROUND

The performer "P" has the audience "A" on all four sides. Ideal intimacy with the audience, however there are limitations as to what kind of set can be used because of site lines. Increased audience reaction. Example: Arena Stage in Washington, D.C.

ENVIRONMENTAL

The audience area and the performing are one. The audience and the performer share the same space. Increased opportunity for interaction and intimacy. Example: Productions including Toni and Tina's Wedding and Tamara.

THE STAGE – THE PERFORMANCE AREA

APRON

The area that can be found between the front curtain of a proscenium stage and the audience.

BACKDROP

The drop farthest upstage on the set. Also a large curtain.

CURTAIN

A solid barrier or fabric curtain, which either moves up or down or pulls back from side to side in a proscenium arch. The curtain is used to conceal the elements of the physical production from the audience such as changes of scenery, passage of time or changes of location. Curtains are most commonly used in theatres with a proscenium format. In addition, not all theatres have curtains.

CURTAIN LINE

The imaginary line across the stage floor that follows the line of where a front curtain would be located.

CYCLORAMA

A large usually white stretch of fabric or curtain that is lit to create setting and masks the rear wall of the stage.

FLATS

Muslin or plywood covered frames used to create walls of a stage set.

FLIES

The area above the top of the proscenium arch usually masked from audience view so that individuals sitting in the seating area cannot see scenery being stored there.

FLY LOFT

The area above the stage where curtains and set pieces are stored and hidden during performance.

GRAND DRAPE

The front, often the decorative curtain of a proscenium stage

LEGS

Narrow curtains in the wings used to mask the back and side stage areas.

MASK

In reference to set design to hide something from audience view.

PLATFORMS

Wooden unites joined together to create floors for a stage set.

TRAP

An opening in the stage floor for characters/actors to pass through for entrances and exits.

STAGE DIRECTIONS

CENTER LINE

An imaginary reference line on the playing area that indicates the exact center of the stage, travelling from upstage to downstage.

CENTER STAGE

The center of the playing (performance) area.

DOWNSTAGE

The part of the stage that is nearest the audience.

STAGE RIGHT AND STAGE LEFT

The right or left of the actor onstage facing the audience.

ONSTAGE

The portion of the playing area visible to the audience.

OFFSTAGE

The area surrounding the playing space not visible to the audience. Typically this refers to spaces accessible to the performers but not the audience, such as the wings and crossovers.

UP STAGE

The part of the stage that is farthest from the audience.

WINGS

Sides of the Proscenium arch stage used for scenery off stage activity or performer entrances and exits.

THE HOUSE AND AUDIENCE AREA

BACKSTAGE

The area behind all the curtains the audience rarely sees.

BACKSTAGE DOOR OR STAGE DOOR

The location of the theatre where performers enter and leave. It is also the location, which audience members may meet performers after the presentation.

BOX OFFICE

The location of the performing arts venue where you can purchase tickets. Most Box Offices have a "will call" window where you may drop off or pick up tickets that have been reserved for you.

DARK

A point in time when all the lights are out on the stage or that the theatre is closed.

ORCHESTRA SEATING AREA

This refers to the seating area located on the main floor of the theatre directly in front of the stage. Orchestra seating is usually the most expensive but offers the best view of the action upon the stage.

ORCHESTRA PIT

Area below the stage that houses an orchestra that is usually placed between the audience and the performance space. Usually found in proscenium arch theaters, this sunken space can be covered when a play does not require a live orchestra. When in use by a full orchestra, the only person the audience can see is the conductor.

ACTING ON STAGE

ASIDE

A line or lines said directly to the audience that other characters in the play cannot hear.

BEAT

A pause of varying length during a scene that is being played out. This beat is usually taken to emphasize emotion or thought or action.

BUILD

To increase tempo of volume or both to achieve a climax within a scene or moment.

CLEAR THE STAGE

A direction given to all actors and technical personnel to vacate the stage prior to the start of a play.

CUE

The last word of dialogue or action signaling the moment for the other actor to speak or move. (SEE PICKING UP THE CUES)

CREATING A CHARACTER

CHARACTERIZATION

The process of creating a character whose words and actions are determined by the elements of the play.

INTNENTION

What the character wants from the other character(s) in a scene

MOTIVATION

The character's reason for doing what he/she does within a moment, scene, act or entire play.

SUBTEXT

The underlying meaning to the scene not always apparent in the dialogue.

PRIMARY CHARACTER

The character that the story is about. "Macbeth" in the play Macbeth

SECONDARY CHARACTER

The Character that serves the story line. Provides information and action. For example, a messenger, butler or confidant

CURTAIN CALL

Usually specifically choreographed arrangement of actors on the stage at the end of performance to acknowledge the applause of the audience.

DICTION

The actor's ability to be understood.

DRESS / TECHNICAL REHEARSAL

A full rehearsal with complete technical accompaniment during the final production phase before an opening night performance.

IMPROVISATION

A scene of any number of characters that is created on the spot using the "who, what, when and where. The actors listen to and respond to one another and create the scene in its entirety or can evolve a scene using a previously arranged scenario.

AD-LIB

Speech or action that is done by the actor within the context of the scene that has not been specifically written or rehearsed.

FOCUS

The place within the performance where the director wants the audience to focus their attention,

FOURTH WALL

An imaginary wall between the actors and the audience.

MONOLOGUE

One character speaking his/her lines either to themselves, another character or the audience.

PICKING UP CUES

When an actor is asked to shorten the time between when a cue is given and his/her response.

PLACES

The direction for all actors and technical personnel to go to their appropriate position and

Be prepared for the start of the play.

PRESENTATIONAL FORMATS

PARA THEATRICAL

Having some qualities of live Theatre but not all. Examples include: mimes, jugglers, street performers, and magicians.

PRESENTATIONAL

When the reality of the audience is the same as the performer. The performer acknowledges and interacts with the audience. Example: Stand Up Comedy, asides.

REPRESENTATIONAL

When the reality of the audience is different than character or performer. The performer does not acknowledge or interact with the audience. Example: Chekhov, Miller, and Ibsen.

RUN THROUGH

An uninterrupted rehearsal of a scene, act or entire play.

SOLILOQUY

A monologue that represents the character's inner thoughts.

STAGE WHISPER

A whisper that is not supposed to be heard by the audience.

STRIKE

Taking down or changing out and removing all set pieces, costumes and props after the completion of a run of a theatre production.

TOPPING A LINE

An actor responding to a line with more volume or intensity than the line before them.

VOLUME

The actor's ability to be heard by all of the audience.

MOVEMENT ON THE STAGE

BLOCKING

The actor's movement upon the stage or when an actor obstructs the view of an actor or action on the stage

CROSS

Movement of an actor from one end of the stage or area to another.

CHEATING

When an actor is opens up the action so that the audience may see the action more clearly.

PANTOMIME

Performing without words, expressing meaning through physical actions/gestures.

STAGE BUSINESS

Small actions performed by an actor, which may enhance character or develop plot.

UPSTAGING

When an actor does business behind another actor or places their body behind another actor forcing the audience or the actor to look the upstage activity.

An act or action, which takes place behind the main action. This draws the audience attention away from what it should be looking at.

TYPES OF PROPS FOR THE STAGE

CHARACTER PROP

A prop that belongs to a particular character such as Sherlock Holmes' pipe.

COSTUME PROP

A prop that belongs to a specific costume such as a whip with a riding costume.

SET PROPS

Those props that belong to a particular set piece (not a character) Example would be a book that might be on a library set.

STAGE PROP

Any particular prop that belongs to a specific set. For example, if a scene took place in an

Antique shop, the antiques would be the stage props.

ELMENTS OF A THEATRICAL PLAY SCRIPT

PLAY SCRIPT

Blue print of what is to be presented on the stage – contains three elements

Action	What physically happens and how the characters move and what they do.
Description:	Describes the characters, story and setting of the play.
Dialogue:	What the characters say – written conversation.

ACT

An organizational division within a play script.

INITIAL INCIDENT

The first most important event in a play. The play develops from this point on.

SCENE

An organizational division in within a script, which is a smaller part of an ACT. Several scenes can make up an ACT.

SETTING

The place where the play occurs

EXPOSITION

The explanation (either verbally or visually) of the who, what, when, where and why of a play.

CLIMAX

The major event in a play or turning point in the story.

RISING ACTION

The series of events following the initial incident and the path of how the story builds toward its climax

FALLING ACTION/DEMNOUEMENT

The series of events that occur after the climax (SEE CLIMAX)

CONCLUSION

The final outcome of the story in the play. The ending.

PROTAGONIST

The play evolves around this character – also known as the "good guy."

ANTAGONIST

The character that forces change or creates conflict against the protagonist – also known as the "bad guy."

ANTI HERO

A person who has both qualities. A bad person who is also good such as "The Godfather," "Batman" or "Dirty Harry."

THEME

The playwright's message

BASIC TERMINOLOGY FOR ON CAMERA ACTING

WHO'S WHO ON THE SET

AD or ASSISTANT DIRECTOR OR FIRST ASSISTANT DIRECTOR

Usually in charge of the crew – runs the set. Keeps order on the set and makes sure that production keeps moving.

ACCOUNT EXECUTIVE

In commercials, this is the person who represents the advertising agency and is the creative force behind the commercial. This person is also the liaison with the actual company or entity representing the product. This could be the fast food company, an auto company or business advertising the good or service.

ART DIRECTOR

In commercial production, this individual or team are responsible for developing all of the visual aspects of the spot including storyboards, drawings and the overall "look" of the spot.

CLIENT

In commercials, the executives who either own or represent the product or service being advertised.

COORDINATOR

In the production of commercials, usually the assistant of the line producer.

CREATIVE TEAM OR UNIT

In commercial production a group of individuals usually made up of The Creative Director, Producer, Art Director, Account Executive and Client.

CREW

Collectively refers to all behind the camera personnel that make up the production unit of the project. Note not all film or television production units will have all of these personnel.

CAMERA OPERATOR

Handles the camera during shooting (single camera) and Dolly Pusher is responsible for moving the camera dolly to a particular location.

CINEMATOGRAPHER

Responsible for setting up all the shots and the ultimate look and feel of the film.

CINEMATOGRAPHY

Camera Assistant – loads film into camera and usually slates.

DESIGNERS

People who create the "universe" of the film or television production - sound, lighting, costume, setting, props,

Special effects.

FOCUS OPERATOR

Responsible for all actors being in focus during shooting. Measures the actual distance from camera to subject.

GRIPS

Responsible for all sets, carpentry, moving lights and equipment.

LIGHTING

Responsible to set and maintain all lighting including generators when on location. Gaffers make sure the required equipment is available and working during production.

MAKEUP ARTIST

Responsible for putting on and maintaining all makeup.

WARDROBE

Responsible for all costumes

DIRECTOR

The person, who provides the point of view for the commercial or film, directs the shots, works with the actors and directs the overall action.

DIRECTOR – FIRST ASSISTANT DIRECTOR

Handles the day-to-day overall details on the set. Keeps the order and flow and makes sure the production keeps moving forward and stays on schedule.

DIRECTOR – SECOND ASSISTANT DIRECTOR

Handle many details of production including: calling actors, setting up actors and keeping the production on schedule.

PRODUCTION ASSISTANT or PA

Does a variety of jobs required for the production of a film, television show or commercial.

PRODUCER

Person responsible for putting together all of the various elements that make up a particular production including budgeting, hiring the director, coordination of all aspects of production including coming up with the idea itself.

SCRIPT SUPERVISOR

Crewmember who reads and times script as it is shot. This person also functions as a continuity person making sure the actors follow the dialogue of the script accurately.

SCREEN WRITER

A person who writes (DESCRIPTION, ACTION, DIALOGUE) in the form of a screenplay to be filmed.

PRODUCTION INFORMATION – WHAT TO KNOW ON THE SET

ACTION

Director's command to start.

APPPLE BOX – Also called WOODEN BOX

A wooden box usually the size of an old fashion apple box which is used for a variety of purposes on a set including: standing to make an actor appear taller, sitting or to adjust to the height of a camera.

BARN DOORS

Metal flaps surrounding the lighting instrument that control the coverage of the light on the action.

BLOCKING THE SHOT

Can be done by the Director or the Director of Photography that carefully works out the movement and actions of actors and cameras. Blocking also takes into consideration lighting and camera focus.

BOOM

A long arm with microphone either held by a production person or attached to a rolling or stationery platform.

BOOTH

For sound, an enclosed soundproof area, separated from crew, with one or more microphones where actors can record the script.

CAMERA LEFT AND CAMERA RIGHT

A direction given by the director or Director of Photography that is orientated from a particular camera's (multi camera) or single camera's point of view.

CAMERA REHEARSAL

Full rehearsal with cameras, lights and other aspects of production to see how it all comes together.

CUE CARD

A card with a portion of the script written on it usually in large letters that is placed near the camera lens so that the actors may read their lines. Cue cards are a common practice in projects such as soap operas, which have large sections of dialogue.

CHEATING

When an actor or object "angles" or faces toward or away from a particular camera to improve the site lines of a particular shot. There is a similar term in Live Theatre that refers to the actor taking a more open position on the stage so that their actions are more visible to the audience.

CUE

Signal in a script to start or stop any type of production activity or action.

CUT

Usually a director's verbal signal to stop the action.

DAILIES aka RUSHES

Usually refers to actual filmed footage as opposed to digital footage, which allows Directors and Director's of Photography to view the footage immediately after shooting. For those films that are actually shot on film, dailies are the film of each day's shooting after it has been developed and printed. These are also known as "rushes."

DOLLY CRANE OR TRIPOD

Wheeled platform that the camera is mounted and can be moved from one location to another.

DRY RUN

Usually refers to a rehearsal without the use of equipment. This type of rehearsal is usually for general blocking or setting up the general action of the scene.

GREEN ROOM

Waiting area for actors (historically painted green).

HIGH HAT

Usually the lowest platform to set the camera. Most of the time this is at floor level.

HITTING THE MARK

For camera focus, a mark (tape) is generally put on the floor to indicate the position of the actor's feet at the end of each move. Actors are expected to move to these marks without looking down at them.

MARTINI SHOT

Hollywood term that describes the final **shot** set-up of the day. According to Dave Knox, author of the film industry slang guide Strike the Baby and Kill the Blonde, the **Martini Shot** was so named because "the next **shot** is out of a glass", referring to a post-wrap drink.

PICK UP

When a director wants to re shoot a small portion of a scene

PLAYBACK

To replay (on a monitor) scenes or takes recorded in the studio.

PRINT IT

A term used when using traditional film that must be processed. When a director is satisfied with a particular take, he/she orders that it be marked and printed. In most contemporary filming situations, directors normally view each take right on the set and mark those that they want to keep. There is no printing involved.

PROPS

PERSONAL – CHARACTER

Objects used by individual actors or characters in a film.

PROPS - SET

Furniture or other objects used for set decoration.

PROPS – COSTUME

Prop that usually belongs to a specific costume – scuba gear, or fox hunting outfit.

ROOM TONE

The actual sound on the set or shoot in total silence.

ROUGH CUT

The first edit of a film, television show or commercial.

RUN THROUGH

Rehearsal from start to finish without stopping

SHOTS - (LARGER TO SMALLER

Shot: Master Shot

*A wide shot that shows the scene in its entirety from start to finish, from an angle that keeps all the players in view. It is often a long **shot** and can sometimes perform a double function as an **establishing shot**.*

Shot: Establishing Shot

Usually the first **shot** of a new scene, designed to show the audience where the action is taking place. It is usually a very wide **shot** or extreme wide **shot**.

SHOT: LONG SHOT

A shot seen from a long distance or framed very loosely.

Shot: Full Shot

A full shot is framed at the feet or beyond.

Shot: Two Shot

Framing of two people.

Shot: Waist Shot

Shot framed at the waist.

Shot: Bust Shot

Shot of a single actor framed at bust.

Shot: Over the Shoulder

A shot in which we look across the back of one actor to the face of the other. Usually done in pairs so that the camera looks at both backs and both actors from similar but opposite points of view.

Shot: Matching

Usually a master shot is done first. The actor must take special care to repeat almost exactly in the over the shoulder shots, close ups and other coverage.

Shot: Close-up (CU)

A shot of the actor's face, object or product taken at close range by the camera.

Shot: ECU

Extreme close-up

Shot: Dissolve

Shot double exposure between two scenes. Usually the first scene is slowly replaced by the second one.

SHOT: FADE DOWN

Previously in another scene and fading down into black

SHOT: FADE UP

Previously in BLACK and fading up into a scene.

SLATE

To identify verbally and visually before each take. A little black board (or white board) upon which essential production information is written (such as title, scene, date and take number.

SPEED

Camera is running properly.

TAKE

Each time you shoot a scene is called a "take".

TELEPROMPTER

Electrical device that displays the script in large letters that rolls by in front of the camera lens at the speed of the actor's delivery.

WRAP – IT'S A WRAP

The end of production or shooting.

ELMENTS OF A SCREENPLAY

SCREENPLAY

Blue print of what is to be filmed – contains three elements

Action   What physically happens and how the characters move and what they do.

Description: Describes the characters, story and setting of the play.

Dialogue: What the characters say – written conversation.

SCENE HEADING

A short description of the location and time of day of a particular scene, also known as a "slug line." For example: **EXT.BOWLING ALLEY-EVE** would denote that the action takes place outside a bowling alley during the night.

ACTION

The physical action and moving images we see on screen.

CHARACTER NAME

When any character speaks, his or her name appears on the line preceding the dialogue. In screenplays, the name is tabbed to a location that is roughly in the center of the line.

DIALOGUE

What the characters says.

EXTENSION

A technical note placed directly to the right of the Character name that denotes HOW the character's voice is heard. For example, O.S. is an extension that stands for Off-Screen.

TRANSITION

A script notation denoting an editing transition within the telling of a story. For example,

CUT TO

The action ends and another scene begins.

DUBBING – ANIMATED AND LIVE ACTION FILMS

ADAPTATION

The script used for dubbing a film into a language other than the original. An adaptation requires every line to be re-written for sync so that the actors' lines match the onscreen performance. Not a translation.

ADR AUTOMATIC DIALOGUE REPLACEMENT

When an actor replaces the voice of another actor or adds voices to a scene after it is shot.

DUBBING

Replacing one voice or dialogue with another. (See also ADR) This dubbing is the process of dialogue replacement in a foreign film, as in dubbing a French voice into English.

FLAP (MOUTH FLAP)

In animation or dubbing, these are the movements of the character's mouth that must be filled by the actor's dialogue.

LIP SYNC

Synchronization of sound and lip movement. (See also ADR and Dubbing)

LOOPING

Providing additional dialogue or sweetening for a scene. Also when an actor has to re-do his/her own dialogue. (See also ADR and WALLA)

M/E

Music and effects added to a production soundtrack.

MNS

Mouth not seen – direction often used in dubbing or voice over where the subject's mouth is not seen in frame.

MOS

A take without sound. Derived from early German Director's "mitout sound."

OFF

Character speaking or reacting is OFF screen.

REAX

Reactions – direction often used in dubbing or voice over.

SWEETEN

To enrich the background often with music, dialogue or sound effects. (See also Looping, ADR and M/E)

SYNC SOUND

Synchronizing sound with picture.

WALLA

A group of actors brought together in the post-production stage of film production to create background dialogue and reactions. Most of Walla does not require "lip sync." However, there may be specific "bits" which appear in a group setting which are normally recorded separately by one of the actors in the group. Walla is a great way to learn film dubbing because you do not have the "lip sync" requirement for a majority of what is being recorded.

VOICE ACTING TERMS

ANNOUNCEMENT

A commercial or non-commercial message. Also referred to as a spot.

ANNOUNCER

The role assigned to a voice-actor that usually has non-character copy. Abbreviated as ANN or ANNC on scripts. Sometimes calls SPOKESPERSON or SPOKES

ARTICULATON

The development and use of clear distinct sounds when speaking dialogue or copy.

BLEED

Extraneous noise coming from the headphones and being picked up by the microphone or from other ambient sources, like other tracks or sometimes over the air radio waves.

BOOM:

An overhead microphone stand.

BOOTH

An enclosed, soundproofed area where voice talent works.

BUY OUT

A one-time payment for voice-over services on a commercial. Common in many non-union situations and industrials, as well as CD ROMs, dubbing, and some non-union looping.

CADENCE

How pauses or emphasis is placed between words that appear in copy.

CALL TIME

The time scheduled for an audition or recording session.

CANS

Another way to describe headphones.

COLOR

Subtle ways to speak or speech nuances that give texture and shading to words to make them interesting and meaningful when reading dialogue or copy.

CONTROL ROOM

Where the engineer and producer often sit. This is usually a separate room from the booth separated by a glass partition.

CUE

An electronic or physical signal given by the director to an actor to begin performing. It can also be cued to a specific time code.

CUT

A specific segment of the voice-over recording, usually referred to during editing.

DEAD AIR

When a voice-over pause is too long or there is a silence in the recording.

DEMO

A demonstration or sample of a voice actor's voice talent.

DISTORTION

Fuzziness or over blown quality in the sound of a recorded piece.

DROP OFF

Not ending strong enough at the end of a word or phrase.

DROP OUT

A minute but deadly moment of silence inside a recorded word or phrase.

EARPHONES

Also known as cans, headphones or headsets.

ECHO

A repetition of sound. Sometimes called futzed.

EDITING

Cutting, adding or rearranging recorded material. Voice elements can be spread apart, slowed down, speeded up, clipped or eliminated to achieve what is required.

EFX:

Effects. Another term for SFX.

ENGINEER

This person who operates the audio equipment during the voice-over session.

FADE IN/ FADE OUT

To increase or decrease the volume of sound.

FALSE START

Situation where a voice actor makes a mistake within the first line or two of copy. The take is usually stopped. It can be picked up or re-slated and done again from the beginning.

FEEDBACK

A distorted, high-pitched sound, usually emanating from headphones or speakers. Many times caused by problems with the console or head-phones getting too close to the microphone.

FOLEY

A special sound stage used for source sound effects. Used to record up-close sound effects for film or video, where the Foley artists match such sounds to picture, such as walking, running, car doors opening or closing, drinking or pulling up a zipper.

FUTZ'

Audio that generally refers to highly processed dialogue effect tracks that make the vocal sound like it's coming from a telephone, a loud speaker, or cockpit of a jet fighter, or whatever the story demands.

GAIN

The volume of a voice, or a fader on the console.

GOBOS

Portable foam like partitions positioned around the actor to absorb or reflect sound.

INFLECTION

The raising or lowering of vocal pitch to underscore the intent or meaning of a word or phrase in the copy.

ISDN:

Integrated Services Digital Network. Special high-quality lines that allow voice recording to be digitally transmitted from one recording facility to another.

JINGLE

A musical commercial.

LEVEL

Usually done before actual recording to set the vocal range of an actor at the optimal volume for recording. When the engineer says, "Let's get a level", the actor will start reading the copy at the level they'll be speaking throughout the spot.

LIBRARY MUSIC

Pre-recorded music that producers use when the budget doesn't allow original music. Each piece of music requires a fee to be paid on a per use basis or such collections can be utilized through an annual subscription fee.

MARKING SCRIPT OR COPY

When an actor places different marks above, below, around, in between and circling words on a script. Best done in pencil, because direction or emphasis may change.

MASTER

The original recording that all future dubs are made from.

MIC

A shortened form of the word mike referring to a microphone.

MIX

The blending of all elements of production including voice, sound effects, music, etc. A final mix usually refers to a completed version of the project.

MONITORS

The loudspeakers located in the control room.

MOUTH NOISE

The clicks and pops a microphone picks up from a dry mouth.

MUSIC BED

The musical soundtrack that will be placed underneath the dialogue or copy or mixed in with it. A bed can also be ambient sounds of a particular environment. For example, a crowded street scene might have a sound bed of people talking as they walk.

OUTTAKE

A previous take that will not be used in the final mix.

OVERLAPPING

When an actor starts his or her line a moment before another actor finishes theirs.

PACE

The speed in which an actor reads copy dialogue. It can also refer to the actual tempo an actor utilizes between cues.

PAPER NOISE

Rustling sound of your script pages that are detected by the micro-phone. The best practice is to set the page on the stand if there is one. You can also clip one page or two pages side by side onto the top of the stand. This will bring the page more to eye level. Try not to touch or move the copy/script pages when recording.

PATCH

To connect or more specifically to create an electrical/digital connec-tion for recording and/or broadcast.

PHASING

When sound reflects or bounces of certain surfaces and causes a weird, disjointed effect in the recording.

PICK-UP

Re-recording a section of a previously recorded take. Usually to "pick up" a word or phrase that the producer or director wants to change with-out re-recording the entire line.

PICK-UP SESSION

A session that is in addition to what has been recorded to do script or copy changes that the producer or director may want done.

PLAYBACK

Listening to what has just been recorded.

PLOSIVE

Any consonant or combination of consonants that causes a popping sound. Usually, "P's" and "B's."

POP

When vocal recordings register to harshly into the microphone. A usual cause of this is when an actor's reading registers too hard when speaking words with plosives.

POP SHIELD

A foam cover set around the microphone or a nylon windscreen in front of the microphone that cuts down on plosives and popping sounds.

PSA:

Public Service Announcement promoting an idea, service or product for the public good. Such as an anti smoking or alcohol abuse campaign.

RESONENCE

The full quality and range of a voice created by vibrations in resonating chambers, such as the mouth and sinus areas.

REVERB

Multiple variations and speeds of echo that can be added to a vocal performance in post production.

ROUGH MIX

As the creative process evolves, this is the step before the final mix. This is when the producer and engineer fine-tune levels of voice, music and sound effects.

RUN-THROUGH

Rehearsing the entire piece before recording. This process allows the producer or director to provide feedback on performance choices.

SFX: Shorthand for sound effects. Also seen as EFX.

SESSION

The block of time set aside where actors, director, engineer and possibly producers record the script of a particular project.

SIBLANCE

An accented or drawn out or excessive "S" sound during speech. Some sibilance is joined with a whistle. This is a very annoying sound, which is easily picked up by the microphone.

SPOT

A commercial or PSA. Originated from the days when all commercials were performed live, in between songs and other programming played on the radio. The performers were considered on the "spot."

STUDIO

The facility where all recording and mixing for a commercial takes place.

SYNC

In dubbing, when an actor must match (lip movements) a voice of a character in animation or live action. It can also mean when an actor matches his or her own lip voice movements from previously shot footage.

TAG

Information placed at the end of a commercial containing a date, time, phone number, website address, legal disclaimer, etc. A different announcer sometimes reads the tag.

TAKE

The recording of one specific piece of voice-over copy or script dialogue. All takes are numbered consecutively, usually slated by the engineer.

TALENT

A broadcast performer, actor, entertainer or voice-over artist.

TALKBACK

Refers to the button connected to the microphone in the engineer's console. It allows the engineer or director to talk to the talent in the booth.

TEMPO

The speed at which copy is delivered.

TIME CODE

A digital read-out on the engineer's console referring to audio and picture positions. Used in film dubbing in order to determine the appropriate placement of vocal tracks.

TONE

A specific sound or attitude.

TRAILER

A commercial or informational segment that promotes a content release.

WAVE FILE

Also known as .wav. A common uncompressed audio file format.

WET

A voice or sound with reverb added to it.

BUSINESS TERMS FOR ACTORS

CASTING DIRECTOR

The person who selects and auditions the performers that most appropriately fit the criteria of a character description or ensemble cast. The Casting Director is usually a contract employee of the production company and is not entitled to receive a commission from the actor if they are cast in a particular role. Has the authority to recommend but not hire an actor for a particular role.

BOOK OUT

When an actor notifies his/her your agent when they are not available for a particular project. They could be out of town or booked for another job.

DIRECTOR

The person, who provides the point of view for the commercial or film, directs the shots, works with the actors and directs the overall action. Has the authority to hire and actor for a particular role.

FIRST REFUSAL

When a producer/director is considering you for an acting job and requests that before you accept another job elsewhere, that they get the right to refuse to hire you first. Often when actors audition for commercials a call-back is usually accompanied with a first refusal.

INDUSTRIALS

Industrial Film. Refers to films made in house for corporations which function as training films, product education, Human resource training, etc.

PRODUCER

Person responsible for putting together all the elements that makes up the production of a film, television production or commercial including: budgeting, selecting the director, coordination of all decisions of personnel involved and makes sure the production is on schedule, also is involved in final editing. Has the authority to hire and actor for a particular role.

REPRESENTATIVES

AGENT

Represents the actor. Acts as salesperson with the actor as the product. An agent is paid a commission of (usually) 10% in exchange for finding the actor work and negotiating the specifics of the actor's employment.

MANAGER OR TALENT MANAGER

A talent representative who guides the actor's career in exchange for a percentage of monies earned. Note: Percentage and length of contracts can vary. Also known as a

Personal Manager or Talent Manager.

RESIDUALS

When actors receive money for the replay either domestically or internationally of their work on a particular Television show, motion picture or commercial. Residuals are tracked by SAG/AFTRA.

RIGHT TO WORK

In a right to work state, companies using the service of actors, cannot refuse to hire someone because they do not belong to a union or do not want to join a union.

Right to work states are: Alabama, Arizona, Arkansas, Kansas, Florida, Georgia, Idaho, Indiana, Iowa, Louisiana, Michigan, Mississippi, Nebraska, Nevada, North Carolina, North Dakota, Oklahoma, South Carolina, South Dakota, Tennessee, Texas, Utah, Virginia, Wisconsin, and Wyoming.

ACTOR'S UNIONS

Unions that govern the working conditions and rate of pay for actors in all mediums. A parent union is the first union that an actor joins. There are several different unions covering specific types of acting work.

ACTOR'S EQUITY ASSOCIATION

Also called Equity, is an American labor union representing the world of live theatrical performance and covers all **live professional stage performance including all**

Broadway shows, regional theatre and touring.

ACTRA

Alliance of Canadian Cinema, Television, and Radio Artists covers all English-speaking performers in Canadian film, television, and radio.

AGVA

The American Guild of Variety Artists (AGVA) represents performing artists and stage managers for live performances in the variety field. The variety area of performance includes singers & dancers in touring shows and in theatrical revues (non-book shows...book revues may be under Actors' Equity jurisdiction), theme park performers, skaters, circus performers, comedians & stand-up comics, cabaret & club artists, lecturers, poets/monologists/spokespersons, and variety performers working at private parties & special events.

SAG/AFTRA

Screen Actors Guild-American Federation of Television and Radio Artists

Covers all acting work on all film and television principal and background performers, journalists, recording artists and radio personalities worldwide.

SPOT

In commercials, the placement of a commercial in different spots and markets around the country other than major markets.

TAFT HARTLEY

When an actor books a union job, a waiver that allows an actor to work on as many union jobs as they want within a thirty day period before being required to join and pay the entrance fee to the union. After the thirty days has passed and the actor is offered another union job, they must join the union first before being allowed to work.

TEST

In commercials, a spot that runs for a limited time in a specific market usually to test the results of the ad. A test can also refer to a "screen test" in which an actor performs a monologue, scene or cold reading within several types of looks on camera for an audition.

AUDITION TERMS

AUDITION

Live or recorded performance showcasing your skills, your physical type and talent toward being cast in a film, television show or play. An audition can be in the form of a cold reading, prepared scene, song or improvisation.

AVAIL

The definition has evolved over time. Originally, in commercial production, it was an understanding between an actor, agent and casting director in which the actor guarantees that the client will have first option on his/her time on specific dates set aside for production. More recently and in practice, it is closer to a partial offer of the acting job when a casting director verifies a particular actor's availability for shoot "if" offered the role for the employment. If the actor agrees to be available for those dates they are put on

"avail." However it is not a guarantee of employment.

BUY-OUT

When an actor is paid a flat fee instead of residuals.

CALL BACK

Request for an actor to come back and read again for usually for the director, producer, art director (in commercials) or writer. Note that a call back does not always have to be for the same role. Actor's can audition for one role and be called back for another.

CATTLE CALL

An audition in which any number of actors may audition for a part on a first come first serve basis. Also called an "open call" or "open audition." Some cattle calls have had hundreds of actors sign up for auditions and are usually not a very productive use of an actor's time.

COLD READING

An audition at which the actor is asked to work from a script or sides without rehearsal.

It should be noted that "cold readings" are rarely cold anymore due to the many

On line services which for a fee, allow actors to download the portions of the script

(SIDES) that will use to audition. This allows the actor additional time to prepare the material and make specific choices for their audition.

CONFLICTS

In commercials, being under contract for two conflicting products (i.e. Tide and Cheer detergents). This is prohibited for union commercials.

COPY

Usually refers to a short script or lines for commercial auditions.

SIDES

A selection of script pages used for auditions usually centered upon a particular character.

CASTING NOTICE TERMINOLOGY

AGE RANGE or RANGE

The age range of the character you will portray generally such as twenties or thirties. This doesn't mean you have to be that exact age. This is not a literal requirement but more about the age range you appear to be when you walk into the casting session.

BREAKDOWNS

An ongoing list of auditions the list projects in all media that are look-ing for actors. Breakdowns include specific character information that Casting Directors send out to agents and managers to help them find the right actors for specific jobs.

EXTRA

Non-speaking atmosphere. Not acting. Also called Atmosphere. These are the people in the background of a scene. While they might appear to be speaking they are not.

NON-SPEAKING

Not necessarily an extra. Usually featured with no dialogue.

OVER 18 TO PLAY YOUNGER

Must be over 18 years of age to play a younger person or child.

TYPE OR CHARACTER TYPE

Term used in casting to describe general character types. Examples are: Street, Generic – Neutral, all American, Ethnic, Hip etc. This also takes into consideration your general demeanor, height, weight, age ranger and general physicality.

UNDER FIVE

A speaking role of less than five lines in taped AFTRA format which cannot exceed 50 words and five lines.

MARKETING FOR ACTORS

BUSINESS CARD

This is an important tool to use when you are meeting new people. It can be a standard card with just your name and contact information. Additionally, it could also have your head shot on it.

COMPOSITES/ZED CARD

Usually used in commercials, this is a black and white or color lithograph printed on two sides. The topside includes a head shot of the actor the backside has anywhere from three to four shots of the actor with several types of looks. One or more of the looks should include a full body shot. (See also head shot)

COVER LETTER

Usually, short letter that accompanies a picture, resume or submission of your reel.

It should say a little something about yourself and identify what you want from the person you have written to.

DEMO REEL

A short sampling (no more than two minutes) of the work you have done. It should highlight short clips of your best performance work and demonstrate your range and capability.

HEAD SHOTS

An 8 x 10 color or black and white picture that serves as the actor's primary marketing tool in obtaining work. This is the first thing that a prospective producer, casting director or agent will see of you. It should look like you and normally have three quarters of the body in the photograph. Can be printed in lithography, glossy, pearl tone or flat. In addition, it can also be uploaded to a particular casting website or distributed through email. (See also Composite)

ON LINE SUBMISSION RESOURCES

Actor's Access:	http://www.actorsaccess.com
LA Casting:	http://home.lacasting.com
Backstage:	http://www.backstage.com
Now Casting	http://nowcasting.com

SOCIAL MEDIA

On line distributors of information – such as Twitter, Facebook, YouTube or your own website or blog. Social media marketing programs usually center on efforts to create content that attracts attention and encourages readers to share it across their social networks.

TEAR SHEETS

Samples of a model's published work (print ads, fashion, advertisements) torn from the publications or printed from the web.

WEBSITE OR LANDING PAGE

Should include photos, current resume, your biography, clips of your work.

PRACTICE MONOLOGUES

The focus of this book is to have you select monologues from a wide selection of material available that can be recommended by an acting teacher, agent, casting director or from on line sources and book stores. The following selection of short monologues is also available for you to use both in acting class and at auditions.

#1   CHEMISTRY

You ever meet someone... ya'know walking down a sidewalk at night, at a party, on an elevator... anywhere? It doesn't matter. And you look at them... and they look at you... and your eyes meet. Then you smile at them and if you're lucky you summon up the nerve to say hello... and then... they say hello right back to you.

(Beat)

It's all very right and you don't want it to end. You want it to begin. But then the moment seems too long... unnatural... and you glance away at something unimportant like your phone or your watch.

(Beat)

Then, you look up again very quickly but they're gone. The moment is over... and you get back to wherever you were going... and you wonder... how it might have been.

#2   CONFESSIONS OF A SERVER

I can't believe it.

The couple sitting at table seven is losing it big time. She just threw a glass of Cabernet in his face and his shirt now looks like a Rorschach test. At the rate they're going, they won't make dessert. I got the whole story when I brought their third round of drinks. She looked up at me and snapped, **"He told me he would divorce his wife – what a crock! That was five years ago!"** I didn't know what to say. Then, she grabbed my arm. **"Do I look like an idiot to you? Well Do I?"** I said, of course not, would you like to hear about our specials tonight?" She just continued. **"Well, he thinks I'm an idiot!"** Then she let him have it. The whole glass of seventeen dollar a glass Cab. For a second, I thought he was going to toss his glass back at her. What can you say when something outrageous like that happens? I smiled politely and said, **"Let me check on your appetizers... I'll be right back."**

(Beat)

Shit.... This job is getting dangerous.

#3   SIGMUND FREUD AND REPRESSION

If I said: "Sigmund Freud?" You would say, "Isn't that the name of that governor of Idaho? Absolutely not! We all know who Sigmund Freud is... he is the father of modern psychology who coined the phrase "repression." Freud believed that repression is an unconscious process in which we exclude unacceptable thoughts and feelings from our own consciousness and memory. We literally block things out that we do not want to remember. Let's see... a thing I don't want to remember? How about that Bugs Bunny raincoat with the floppy ears my mother forced me to wear on the very first day of school in second grade? I really don't want to remember that.

(Beat)

Boy, Freud hit the repression nail right on the head with a sledgehammer... and he never even met my mother.

#4 GROUPS

Okay, you want me to say it? I'll say it. ***"I'm a loner!"*** I'm not a group type of person. I don't like to talk to other people. It's not like I don't like people... they're okay. But the truth is I really don't care what they think or whether or not they like or dislike me.

(Beat)

It's actually very freeing. I don't want to spend on tiny moment contemplating what other people think about me. Even you... I hope you're not offended... I just like it better this way... it leaves more time for me... more time to think about me.

(Beat)

Where are you going?

(Beat... now alone in silence.)

Now, where was I?

#5 WEARING GLASSES

What is it about wearing glasses that make the people who wear them appear to be smarter? Does the logic go "if you wear glasses, you read more and therefore…? (You know the rest). Even worse, if the glasses being worn are very thick, it implies that the person wearing them is a genius. Is this a load or what?

(Puts on glasses) Now there's another way to think about this. "You wear glasses and actually "feel" smarter. Let's see, I just put these on and I suddenly feel… "Clever." Go ahead, ask me something. Stock tip? Politics? American History? Anything you want except math or driving directions. I would need a thick pair of glasses to answer a math question. Really, I don't do math or directions. You don't need either of them anyway. We have calculators for math and well… Guys just don't ever ask for directions. It's not masculine to ask someone how to get somewhere. Guys have an intuitive sense of location at all times. It's part of our "hunting" heritage. Lastly, I am one of those people who always knows *exactly* where they are going. Always.

(Beat)

So, fire away… ask me anything you like.

(Beat)

I'm waiting. Nothing? I would like to stay and talk but I am my way to the library to read some very thick books. Now, if I can only remember how to get there?

#6   LUCKY

I always thought a name like "Lucky" would be great name for a stray dog that had been rescued from doggy death row and given a home. People would say, ***"Wow, look at that stray dog now... living the good life... boy he's really lucky."*** Then, I met this guy at a party last week whose name was Lucky. At first I figured he was just playing with me when he told me his name. But everyone that saw him said stuff like ***"Hey Lucky What's up?"*** and ***"How are you doing Lucky!"*** I figured the guy was telling me the truth. His name was really ***"Lucky."*** Seemed like a cool person who said he was going to law school after college. Then I thought law school is super hard to get into, so Lucky was either "Lucky" or "Very smart." Then, I thought about his chosen profession. How would the world look upon an attorney named Lucky? What if the fact that being called "Lucky" by everyone might actually give him bad luck? I mean, what if everything Lucky touched turned to crap? How would that work? With a name like "Lucky," there would always be the never-ending pressure to come out on the top of things all the time. Otherwise, you wouldn't be lucky. Right? People would say, ***"What's the matter Lucky? Not so "lucky" today? We'll better luck next time..."*** The truth of it is when I hear the name "Lucky," I still think it's a dog's name... a stray dog. Also, I also think of "Lucky" in Pokémon. When Lucky becomes a lawyer... that could be a problem as well. Wonder if anyone else will think of that?

#7 IRON CITY
1957 COUNTRY SQUIRE

When I was a kid, I used to ride in the back of my dad's station wagon – a 1957 Ford Country Squire. It was mostly white on the outside with wood panels along the doors and white walled tires. Inside, all-vinyl seats in a red-and-white pleated pattern. Every once in a while, my dad would fold down the rear seat, which made the car feel more like a bowling alley than a car. I mean, there was lots of room to roll around. Cars were much bigger back then or maybe it was that I was much smaller. I'm not sure if seat belts were invented yet, but I don't remember ever wearing one. All I knew was when the back seat was folded down; the car seemed larger than life and full of possibilities; like an intergalactic space ship, a B17 bomber and with the help of a small plaid blanket or my favorite a submarine. However, my all time favorite thing to do was to just lie on my back and watch the world upside down through the rear window. The world was connected at different angles. Trees, clouds, black wires and telephone poles all looked much better upside down. The ground had a way of defining everything the same way; but when you viewed the world upward through the rear window of our Country Squire, upside down trees danced lightly under a blue sky with the never ending sway of black power lines. As the AM radio played *"One Two Three, Look at Mr. Lee"* by the Bobbettes, I pulled the blanket over my head and slowly went to periscope depth.

#8   KONG ISLAND 1931

(The sound of distant drums)

Musta been maybe 300 hundred of these primitive types running around a large fire wearin nothin but their wholesomes screamin war woops to a drum beat louder than hell. We moved up on em real slow. I says to Joey in a soft whisper, "Joey, shake a leg will ya? Take that camera outta the sack and set up real steady on that rock over yonder there... then when I give you the one finger cue... that's when you start to crank away and when I use my hand here at my throat like a knife... that means cut... okay?" He nods and works his way up on the rock and then I give him the cue to start crankin, which he does. He's getting lots of swell footage of this native chief with a monkey mask dancing around the fire. These natives here, were the real McCoy no cigar store tom-tom beatin fakers. Then, all of a sudden like, the drums stop cold and we there's the whole lot of em lookin right at us like we're meat on a stick! I give Joey the cue to cut with my hand like this... ya'know movin my hand across my neck like a knife but Joey keeps cranking the camera. I did the only thing I could, the 23 skidoo! I run like crazy to the boat and barely get out alive. Look here at this scar, it's from a spear one of them there savages threw at me. Joey hid the camera under a rock, dove in the water and made a swim for it. I though he was a goner... be he made it back to the boat... and now everything's just swell! We're gonna go back and get the camera and the film tonight while the little devils are all sleeping. I just can't wait to see what's on the other side of the great big wall they got running across the island. Maybe we'll head on over there too and see what all that monkey dancin fuss is all about.

#9   ATROPHY

I'm so glad you could all come on such a short notice. I wanted all of us to get together today, as a group and have a conversation collectively about the conversation that we will have when we meet next Thursday. I thought it would be productive to talk about what we would talk about next week. ... and I know that Stephen wanted to discuss today a "sub set" of this idea. But after our pre meeting discussion we have agreed to table his ideas until Tuesday at 10:00 AM. We can hold that meeting in this conference room as well. As you can see, we have to discuss setting up a specific agenda for Thursday and if we have time to today to put that agenda in an appropriate order... Okay, now that I have detailed the framework of our discussion... who would like to go first?

#10 BRUISE ON MY THROAT

I'm so sorry, I really should be here… there's nothing wrong with me. I don't know why I came in the first place… an emergency room is for people who are really hurt or really sick… and I'm… I'm okay. This bruise on my throat is really nothing… it's actually my own fault… no big deal. See we were talking… just talking and then we sort of got into an argument… next thing I know is I scratched his face with my hand. So you see it was all my fault. I shouldn't have done that. All he did was grab me by the throat to protect himself… that's all. And this bruise on my rib here… isn't from a kick. He just sort of tripped over me when I fell on the floor. He didn't kick me or anything. It was totally an accident.

(Beat)

So, it's all going to be all right, okay… it's just a small bruise on my throat… so I'm just going to go home now… okay?

(Beat)

Please forget that I ever came in here.

#11 THINGS I DON'T DO

Things I don't do...

Valet Park my car...

Shake hands when I first meet someone.

Step into an elevator with someone with obnoxious smelling perfume. Or worse...

Sit in a movie theatre next to someone with Pantene hair gel.

Wait in line for anything more than two minutes.

Put salt on my food before I taste it...

Put my shoes on... left foot first

Step on the cracks on the sidewalk when I walk.

Go to a circus... especially one that has clowns or elephants that do tricks.

Ask for autographs from movie stars...

Pick up or pet a snake.

Eat cotton candy or snails.

Walk in the rain with an open umbrella.

Trick or Treat on Halloween... or give presents for Christmas... that's Santa's job.

Put milk in my coffee... or tea... or anything.

Put a penny instead of a quarter in a parking meter...

Walk in Central Park between midnight and two AM... singing "I'm in the Money..."

And most important of all... Say goodbye... to anyone when I leave them.

(Beat, then exit.)

#12 FIVE SMALL BITES

One great way to lose weight is to just take five small bites of whatever you're eating when you're eating and then.... here's the hard part... put the fork down and wait at least two minutes before picking up the fork again. When you pick it up again, you do five more bites. You can mix or match whatever you eat but all you can do is five bites... then two minutes with the fork down... How do you know when two minutes goes by? Easy sing Twinkle Twinkly Little Star to yourself twice and you should be good to go.

(Beat)

So, what's the science here? Don't know... don't care. I think I read somewhere, that by slowing down your intake, you get full faster. It literally, gives your stomach a chance to send a message to your brain that says, **"I've had enough... don't send anything else down here..."** That's why you have to wait the two minutes -- because your stomach takes a little more time send a message to your brain. Or maybe, we're so busy counting and singing to ourselves that we forget to eat. Who knows? Who cares...? I'll tell you what I **do** know, Sheila at my Ti - Bow Boot Camp Cardio Crash Class does it and she is as thin as a string bean... she also may be anorexic but let's not get caught up in all the details. Just do the five small bites... I promise you, it will work... and that's all that matters. Don't forget... just five small bites. Okay?

Right.

Gotta go...

#13 THE PLUMBER

See, the problem you got here is that you're going in with one inch and then right there when pipe hits the foundation you go down to half inch and half inch is no good. You can't get enough pressure with half inch. To do this job right, we gotta come here with two inch, then here, if you wanna save, we can do one inch. But, you gotta do it in copper. Now you don't have to do copper if you wanna save a few bucks. Copper right now is very dear. I mean, I can get it but you're gonna have to fork out some bucks. But when you go copper, you're going for life here. If you wanna save, we can lay PVC, and PVC is fine and all but it doesn't have the same stayin power like copper. The question is, how long you gonna be here? If you're just passin… I meant, "passin through" not passing away…. then we'll go PVC. If you're going be here a while, then I'd go copper. Spend the money and enjoy the copper… you know what I mean? There's nothing like copper pipes. If we do the job, I would do the uppers too. Run the line in from the main and go right through to the uppers. You're probably lookin at five maybe ten grand. Could be a little more because I don't know what we're gonna find when we get into it. There may be some bugga boo's under the house here, we can't see right now. If we run into a bugga boo, then we gotta deal with it. Can't do it half-assed. Right? If you wanna go PVC, we can do that. I wouldn't do it for nothing but it's your house. Am I right? PVC is good for the garden. Like sprinklers and such. But under the house… you gotta go copper.

#14 BIOLOGICAL MATURATION

I was waiting on the eight items only checkout line at the grocery store, when I leaned just one step to the right, like this (move to the right), to get a pack of breath mints. Then, stepped back again and BOOM! The woman that was behind me was now in front of me putting her Slim Quick Yogurt and Diet six-pack on the checkout counter. I was just about to say something to her when she (without looking up at me) barked: *"Sir, while you're there, can you reach over on that rack and get me a package of breath mints?"* Without thinking, I replied, *"Spearmint or Lemon?"* Counting her yogurts with her index finger, she replied, *"No, winter mint. Now you've made me lose count."* I apologized: *"I'm so sorry, doesn't seem that they have..."* She let out a breath: *"Forget it then... I'll just have to get by without them."* She turned away from me as she inserted her credit card into the chip slot. That's when I decided to let her have it. *"Miss or Madam whatever you are... you just cut in front of me in line. Now, that was insensitive and rude."* She stopped what she was doing and turned back toward me and gave me a piercing look: *"Are you absolutely positive that there are no winter mints on that rack? You think you could check again? They've got to be there!"* I visually fumbled through the rack again... through the candy bars and rawhide chew sticks... not a winter mint in sight. Before I could answer, she shook her head in disappointment, picked up her plastic bag and left. At that moment, I knew I had reached the true apex of "Biological Maturation." I had become invisible.

#15 MY LOCH NESS

You moved silently through the still dark water like a dream spun by Hypnos spirit.

In the soft glow of the starlit sky I could see your Aphrodite smile and silken hair that fell lightly upon your Madonna neck.

Such beauty so rightly kept, can beguile a mind's admonitions to soften in favor of a heart's desire.

As if affection's gaze were a madness,

I turned toward you to speak, but you were gone.

I found only blackness and night silently reveling upon themselves some darker fantasy too quiet to be heard.

I find myself at an apparition's end a plaintive seeker longing to see you just once more.

My Loch Ness

#16 BABYSITTING

My parents have been on my case about being responsible and all that and about getting some sort of part time job after school. Well, I tried the job interview thing. I went to the mall last Tuesday and walked around a little, but didn't see anywhere I wanted to work. I mean how can you work in the mall anyway? The mall is a happy place... not for working... no way... it's for hanging out. Right? Then I went to In & Out Burger, Starbucks and Forever 21 but nothing! The kid that interviewed me at Starbucks asked for my number! Gross! The rest said that they didn't need anyone with my experience. I don't get it... I don't have any experience. I guess the economy is kind of bad right now. So, I finally decided to get a babysitting job watching little Oscar here. It's pronounced "OS... CAR" His parents are really fussy about that. But it's not so bad, except occasionally little OS CAR gets a bit fussy... like now! And the only way to get him quiet is to talk to him in a really high voice. (High voice) *Like this! There you go... have a little baby food Os Car. It's peach your favorite flavor. Here it comes! Just like a giant dinosaur flying in the sky!*

SWAHCK! SWAHCK! SWAHCK!

Flying Pterodactyl coming in.... dropping lots of nice peach baby food for little OS CAR! Here it comes!

YEOW!

(Beat)

Oscar... you closed your mouth at the last minute... why did you do that? Now I have to Maybe I should rethink this whole "babysitting" thing and check out the mall again.

#17 BRIDGES

I built a bridge to you every time you pulled away from me. Whenever you became cold and distant and I reached out to you and pulled you back in. That's the way it has been for a long time.

But now, I am tired of doing all the work. Your distance is wearing me down. I'm starting to give in and feeling maybe that you and I staying together may not be worth it. Just so you know, the next time you go distant on me, I'm going to let you go. I am not going to fill in the silence any more with smiles and warm touches, which are not returned.

If you go distant, it will be what it is – just an empty space between us. There'll be no bridge to connect us from where we have been to what we may become. There will be nothing to hold us together to stop us from being apart... except ourselves.

#18 VOICE MAIL GREETING

Hello, I am busy or talking on my cell right now making the world a better place. Saving the planet, rescuing fur-baring creatures like dogs and cats from harm. It's not that I don't like reptiles or birds, but fur-baring animals are the most oppressed by their human masters. If this is George, please leave the keys under the mat and remember it's not your fault. It's really my fault we didn't work out. I find it almost impossible to commit to anyone longer than thirty days. Also, I don't want you to think I have anything against employees of the U.S. Postal Service or don't want you to deliver my mail any longer. I have a phobia of uniforms, which is rooted, to my childhood parochial school experience. I'm not saying anything perverse happened to me in Catholic school. However, what I am saying is that there is a conflict between my intellectual and spiritual self. And George, this doesn't mean we can't still be friends and go to the Woody Allen film festival together as long as you don't mind skipping *Annie Hall*. I absolutely will not sit through the kitchen scene with the lobster.

As, for the rest of you, that are **"not George,"** please speak slowly, leave your name and number and I will get back to you as soon as humanly possible. Oh, almost forgot, if this is Dr. Woo at Izzy Zen Acupuncture Aroma Therapy Spa, I can't do next Tuesday because I will be on a vegan retreat upstate. When you hear the beep, you know what to do – Bye!

(Exit)

#19 HELLO

First of all, I just want you to know, I've never done an Internet date before... this is my first. I just find it utterly impossible to meet anyone... it's all so contrived. Please have a seat. There, doesn't that feel better? Good. Now about your "hello." First and foremost, I want to tell you that I am very uncomfortable with saying "Hello" right off. Really, we hardly know one another and I would not expect such familiar behavior from someone I just bump into on the street. At first blush, I can easily say that I really like you at least what I know of you. You do look a bit younger in your photo but I'm willing to overlook that detail. But here we are... I think it is always a good idea for two individuals, such as we, to take their time and to know one another as fully as possible before moving forward.

(BEAT)

I can sense by your closed physicality and the way you are avoiding direct eye contact that you are not enthralled by our conversation. I'm looking for someone who knows where they're going in life...

(Beat no answer)

So, here we are. What shall be our next step?

(Beat)

You are getting up. That is a start. Now, you are walking away... that is a positive physical action. That is definitely a choice... Going... Going.... Going...Gone.

(Silence)

... and we were doing so well?

#20 THE SOLILOQUY

(Holding skull or other profound object)

To be... or...

(Beat)

Line...

(Whisper) "or..."

Or...Not...

Line...

(Impatient whisper) "to..."

Right... Can I try this again? Okay here goes.

To be... or not...

Line.

(Irritated Whisper) "To be or not to be... **that** is the question."

I didn't ask for the line **"that is the question."** So you shouldn't have given it to me because it makes me look like I don't know my lines. I really **do** know my lines but just don't feel comfortable getting up in front of people and reciting them. I mean... I **had the lines** when I was driving in my car on the way here. Am I going to get a low grade on this? I really need an "A" in this class... and I really do know my lines... so it's really not fair if I get a low grade! I mean I'm really trying...

(Beat)

Again? All right, I just want to take a moment to get into character.

(Beat, closing eyes and relaxing shoulders then exhale)

Okay, here goes…

(British dialect)

To be…! or not to be…. really a question I shan't answer? Whether it is bolder to buffer the slings and marrow of outrageous misfortune wretch-edly ripped timely from my womb. My fire burneth….and my caldron… bubbleth. And yet, a rose by any other name is still pretty much a rose… so go figure? But hence… what of it?

Shall I say fi…? Shall I say fo…? No, rather… I shall say… *Nay*… we are all but gay players who strut and fret their stuff upon the stage in joyous proclamation *"June busteth out all over…. all over the meadow and the hill!"*

(Beat)

Scene!

(Beat)

I told you I knew it.